Operating in the Gift of the Teacher:
A Practical Biblical Guide

By

Dr. Ceretta A. Smith

Foreword

It is so awesome to be called as a 'Doma Gift' in the body of Christ in these last days; especially, those that posses the call of the <u>Teacher</u>. The **call to teach** carries a passion that keeps one on the thralls of creating ways to communicate a point and it wakes one up in the middle of the night. It also makes one to search the Bible and the concordance in order to find out what something means while knowing that if you do not, sleep will be almost impossible to achieve that night. That call that Jesus was so often noted for was before the discovery of His Messianic identity! Oh, to serve in that place and to see the Savior change the listener's posture is euphoric to say the least.

I was so excited to read and experience **Operating in the Gift of the Teacher!** In this book, Dr. Ceretta Smith explains the function of the **Teacher** in and for the body of Christ with such zeal and simplicity that is causes the reader to rekindle the fire and for those that may have journeyed from a labor of love into a weary worker; or to connect those to that <u>operating gift</u> that had so long eluded them.

Dr. Smith is an extraordinary woman of God who has shown a fierce dedication to the King and her family. It is not unusual that the Father would choose her hands to pen His heart for this generation. As a Kingdom Pastor/Teacher for over 24 years, I revel in the birthing of this book and I excitedly look forward to making it a part of our ministry development curriculum and I recommend that others do as well.

Graciously,
Dr. C. Andre Johnson
Senior Pastor, Victory Community Church-AZ

Dedication

This book is dedicated to my Mom; a virtuous woman and great teacher to not only me but many, many other women. You have and continue to touch the lives of more people than you know. You are my "HERO" and I love you more than words can convey.

Operating in the Gift of the Teacher:
A Practical Biblical Guide

Unless otherwise indicated, all scriptures are quoted from
the King James Version of the Bible.

Published by: **To His Glory Publishing Company, Inc.**
463 Dogwood Drive, NW
Lilburn, GA 30047
(770) 458-7947
www.tohisglorypublishing.com

This Book is available at:
Amazon.com, BarnesandNoble.com, Booksamillion.com,
UK, Canada, Australia, etc.

Also, see the Order Form at the back of this book or call/email below to order this book.

Email: tohisglorypublishing@yahoo.com
(770) 458-7947
www.tohisglorypublishing.com

ISBN: 978-0-9854992-1-1

Table of Contents

Preface

I have always considered myself to be a studious person and always carried an above average GPA. Excellence in the area of academics is something that I have always strived for. But, there is something about the Word of God that intrigues me like nothing else. I am pulled and drawn to it and I could study it all day long. I love to dig into the Word of God and look for those hidden truths of His Word. I often have "ah hah" and "wow" moments" and the feeling of having God reveal something to me is indescribable.

But it does not stop there for me, I not only love to study and search the Word of God, but when I do, I want to tell everybody what God has shown me. I am sure co-workers present and former, family and close friends will attest to this. Whenever God drops something on me, I bubble with excitement and I always immediately look for someone to pass the information on to; especially those that may be in the dark about a particular subject.

Ignorance is a pet peeve of mine and I know that it is a tool the enemy loves to use to keep people in bondage, so no matter where I go or what I do, I always find myself sharing the Word of God with someone and breaking it down for them. **I taught my first official Bible Study in 2000 at the Chapel in Schweinfurt, Germany and it was on the subject of Love. Little did I know the gift of "Teaching" was birthed in me that very night!**

Even after my teaching and as I grew in my Christian walk, I still did not hear a lot about the **gift of Teacher** in the Body of Christ and did not consider myself a **"Teacher."** I noticed that great emphasis was placed on the other <u>five-fold ministry gifts</u>, but that of the **Teacher** seemed to be overlooked and not developed in those who had it. But, my gift made room for me because **the Holy Spirit is the best Teacher you could ever have.**

Being a military family, we transitioned almost every three to five years, so from ministry to ministry I continued to teach when the opportunities presented themselves; whether it was a Bible study, a workshop for leaders in the house or how to dress your body shape to our women's ministry. I gleaned from those that stood before me and I used them as models of how to do and what to do, but most importantly, I relied on the Holy Spirit to walk me through it each time I had to teach. I did this because I know that that Word of God said in **Zechariah 4:6** that, *"It is not by might or by power but by my spirit."*

It was not until 2006 that God began to upgrade me in the gift of Teaching. I had joined Calvary Deliverance and Apostle Brenda Colbert who is one of the Teachers in the house had a very unique teaching style. I had not seen anyone teach the way that she did because she was very interactive and really engaged her audience. Even the least among us could comprehend what she was teaching. I also plugged into Glory of Zion in Corinth, Texas and I began to really pattern myself after

Robert Heidler. <u>I learned so much from him and I began to incorporate some principles from his techniques in my teaching</u>. I will discuss these principles and techniques later on in this book. I have never met him, but I consider him a mentor and hope to someday meet him.

Nevertheless, I was identified and brought on board in the church as a teacher and I was challenged in this area to grow to another level of excellence and to make sure the people got it; all the people, from the youngest to the oldest. Not only did God begin to polish the gift and is still polishing it, but I began to get a greater understanding of the **gift of the Teacher** and this has allowed me to flow in the grace of the teaching gift at another level.

As I stated when I started out teaching, I did not have a "Manual or Practical Guide" in my hand. Therefore, it was truly trial and error time for me but the Holy Spirit was teaching me and helping me to correct my errors. **Now, I am so thankful for leaders that recognized my gift of the Teacher and that began to instruct me or teach me by pouring their wisdom into me to bring me to the next level of my growth.**

It is my prayer that this guide will give you the foundation you need or build upon the foundation that has already been laid so that you are able to teach God's people with the meat of His Word with, excellence, simplicity, life and enthusiasm. It is also my prayer that you come to better understand the **gift of the Teacher** as it relates to the <u>five-fold ministry gifts</u> and that you are better able to step into God's purpose for your life as a **Teacher** in full force. God Bless you. The Body of Christ needs your gift!

—**Ceretta Smith**

Acknowledgements

Lord thank you for every gift that you have given me and for causing me to know and understand that they are not for me alone but for Your people and for Your GLORY! I love You with every fiber of my being and dedicate my life to doing Your will in the earth.

Thank you to every Five-fold Ministry Gift that has impacted my life and enhanced my spiritual growth. Without your prayers, support, guidance, fathering and mothering, I truly would not be where I am today!

To my best friend; my husband **Sterling Smith**, thank you for listening, for your counsel and for all of the things big and small that you do for the boys and me. You are a "GEM" and truly a blessing to my life. I love you!

Lesson 1
Who Is The Teacher?

God Set the Gifts in the Church

Who is the **Teacher** is a good place for us to start. Throughout scripture, references are made to teachers but our focus is going to be on the five-fold ministry gift and office of the Teacher as referenced in **1 Corinthians 12: 27-28** and **Ephesians 4: 11**:

1 Corinthians 12:27-28:

> "Now ye are the body of Christ, and members in particular. And God hath set some in the church, first apostles, secondarily prophets, thirdly teachers..."

Ephesians 4:11:

> "And he gave some, apostles; and some, prophets; and some, evangelists; and some, pastors and teachers;"

According to the text above, God Himself set in the church firstly apostles, secondarily prophets and thirdly teachers and so forth and so on. And each of these gifts has a specific purpose and function within the church. They have been set in the church for a reason. If you read a little further in **Ephesians 4:12**, He defines His purpose for giving these five gifts in the church:

Ephesians 4:12:

> "For the perfecting of the saints, for the work of the ministry, for the edifying of the body of Christ:"

According to verse 12, the function and purpose for these five ministry gifts is to prepare the people of God for works of service so that the body of Christ will be built up. God did not give these five leadership gifts to the body for them to do the work; but rather for them to enable the people of God to do the work of the ministry.

So in the text above, we see clearly that the Teacher is listed as one of these gifts. I wanted to make this clear because in Colossians 3: 16, we are all admonished to teach, and we are told that all believers should be able to teach the basics of the Gospel to some degree. As a result, it must be clearly understood that the ministry gift of the **Teacher** is one who brings instruction to the Body at large. **The Teacher has a divine call, gift and anointing into the five-fold ministry.**

Combination of "Giftings"

There are combinations of other "giftings" that most likely will be active in the office of the **Teacher** as well; such as <u>teaching</u>, <u>exhortation</u>, <u>organization</u>, <u>word of wisdom</u>, <u>word of knowledge</u>, <u>prophecy, etc</u>. **So, the question is; who is the Teacher? The answer is the Teacher is a five-fold ministry gift set in the Church by God to help equip and train the people of God so that the body will be built up.** If that is you hold on, there's more in the chapters to come.

Lesson 1 Notes

Ceretta Smith

Lesson 1 Notes

Lesson 2
What Does The Teacher Do?

Duties of the Teacher

In the previous chapter, I revealed to you that the Bible makes references to teachers throughout scripture, but that our focus was that of the five-fold ministry gift —the **Teacher.** I want to go back and look at the other references to teachers so that we can get a clearer picture of the five-fold ministry gift of the Teacher and what the **Teacher** does as opposed to the other gifts.

In **Titus 2:3-5**, the older women are admonished to teach the younger women:

> "³**The aged women likewise, that they be in behaviour as becometh holiness, not false accusers, not given to much wine, <u>teachers of good</u> <u>things</u>.**

> ⁴**That they may teach the young women to be sober, to love their husbands, to love their children,**

> ⁵**To be discreet, chaste, keepers at home, good, obedient to their own husbands, that the Word of God be not blasphemed."**

The "Kalodidaskalo" Teacher

To **teach** here is the Greek word **Kalodidaskalos** which means **teacher of good things or teaching what is good.** These women are indentified as teachers but not as the five-fold ministry gift Teacher. They are to teach the younger women in the areas of dress, caring for their homes, raising their children and so forth.

Today these women might be identified in the body as your "Church Mothers." Not to say that a "Church Mother" cannot be called to the five-fold gift of **Teacher.** When this is the case, the dual gifting will be noted and in that instance, the **Teacher's** audience will not just be limited to a local church per say but the audience will encompass a larger sphere of authority.

I want to mention here that a "Church Mother" is not the only person the scripture above is referencing. For example, I was mentored and 'discipled' by many women who were not older than me in terms of a chronological number, but were more mature and well seasoned. As a result, they had a lot to pour into me in the areas of being a good mother and wife.

Also, in **Acts 5:34**, we see the word **teacher** again:

> "Then one in the council stood up, a Pharisee named Gamaliel, a *teacher* of the law held in respect by all the people, and commanded them to put the apostles outside for a little while.

The "Nomodidaskalos" Teacher

This man is identified as a **teacher of the law**. This is the Greek word **Nomodidaskalos** which means **a doctor of the law or a teacher of the law.** According to Barnes Notes on the Bible, "this teacher was a teacher of the Jewish Law." His office was one that was in place to interpret the laws of Moses and to preserve and communicate the traditional laws of the Jews.

Again, we see the difference in function from that of the five-fold gift of **Teacher. This teacher taught strictly to the Jews concerning Jewish law and tradition.** And lastly in **2 Peter 2:1**, we see the word **teachers** used again:

> "But there were false prophets also among the people, even as there shall be false teachers among you, who privily shall bring in damnable heresies, even denying the Lord that bought them, and bring upon themselves swift destruction."

The "Pseudodidaskalos" Teacher

Here, the reference to the word is the Greek word **Pseudodidaskalos** which means **false teachers.** There is a great deal of false teaching going forth in the Church today and many are being deceived but I believe that even as God is setting the **Apostles** and **Prophets** in their rightful places, He is also setting **Teachers** in their rightful places as well. A vital part of this is that He is separating those who have the **divine call** to the office of **Teacher**.

The "Didaskalos "Teacher

Now that we have looked at the other capacities in which one can be called a

teacher, let us look at the five-fold ministry gift of the office of the **Teacher** and what this person has been called to do. Let us look at **Ephesians 4:11**:

> **"And he gave some, apostles; and some, prophets; and some, evangelists; and some, pastors and <u>teachers</u>."**

And also **Corinthians 12:28**:

> **"And God hath set some in the church, first apostles, secondarily prophets, thirdly teachers, after that miracles, then gifts of healings, helps, governments, diversities of tongues."**

The **Teacher** in the verses above is the Greek word **Didaskalos** that means:

1. A teacher

2. In the NT one who teaches concerning the things of God and the duties of man;

    a. one who is fitted to teach

    b. the teachers of the Jewish religion

    c. of those who by their great power as teachers draw crowd around them i.e., john the Baptist and Jesus

    d. the preeminence used of Jesus by Himself as one who showed men the way to salvation

    e. of the Apostles and of Paul

    f. of those who in the religious assemblies of the Christians undertook the work of teaching with the special assistance of the Holy Spirit.

    g. master (Jesus)

    h. doctor

Dictionary.com defines **teacher** as **one whose occupation is teaching others, a person who teaches and instructs.**

The "Didasko" Teacher

To **teach** in the Greek is the word **Didasko,** it is where we get the English word **Didactic** and it means:

1. To teach here means;
    a. to hold discourse with others in order to instruct them or to deliver didactic discourses
    b. to be a teacher
    c. to discharge the office of a teacher or to conduct one's self as a teacher

2. To teach one as in to;
    a. impart instruction
    b. instill doctrine into one
    c. the thing taught or enjoined
    d. to explain or expound a thing
    e. to teach one something

The definitions of **teacher** and **teach** in both Greek and English make it clear what the function of this gift is; that is, to teach and instruct the people of God in the truths of His Word by teaching sound doctrine so that they will be established in their faith and be equipped for effective service in the Church. But that is not all the Teacher does. **Let us look at some more scriptures and dig a little deeper into the functions and purpose for the Teacher aside from those listed above.**

The "Didaskalos" as Master

In the synoptic Gospels, you will find that the word **Didaskalos** is also translated as **Master** and they all make reference to Jesus in these texts. Jesus was and is the only man to walk the face of the earth that operated in all of the five-fold ministry gifts. This is how He was able to give this gift as it was one dimension of what He did — teach.

Jesus was able to give what He had in Himself to others and this in itself is a lesson for us because we cannot give what we do not have. We will talk about Jesus as our greatest

example of a Teacher in another a chapter. The next reference to **Teacher (Didaskalos)** can be found in **Acts 13: 1-3:**

> **"Now there were in the church that was at Antioch certain prophets and teachers; as Barnabas, and Simeon that was called Niger, and Lucius of Cyrene, and Manaen, which had been brought up with Herod the tetrarch, and Saul.**

> **²As they ministered to the Lord, and fasted, the Holy Ghost said, Separate me Barnabas and Saul for the work whereunto I have called them.**

> **³And when they had fasted and prayed, and laid their hands on them, they sent them away."**

The Teacher as Part of Leadership

Here we get our first glance of the New Testament **Teachers** and what they did in addition to teaching. The **Teacher** has the spiritual ability to take the truth of God's Word and explain it to the people in a manner that they can understand it and apply it to their day to day living. Here in Acts 13:1-3 above, we see another dimension of what a **Teacher** does. In this text the **Teacher** is numbered among the leaders that were at Antioch. They were a part of a team of leaders that was ministering to the Lord by fasting and they heard from the Lord. We see here that along with the Prophets, they also laid hands on those that the Holy Spirit said to separate.

The Lifestyle of the Teacher

From the scripture above we see that first, they were ministering unto the Lord; this speaks to **a lifestyle of worship.** A Teacher has a passion for not only the Word of God, but a passion for the presence of God. As **Teachers**, it is easy for us to get caught up in studying alone; I know that I can study for hours and hours but we have to have a balance because information and knowledge alone are not enough. What you study or learn has to be watered by the anointing. Therefore as **Teachers**, if no one else on the team is up in a worship service, we should be! **The reason is because, as our worship ascends revelations descends** and this will allow us to flow in a dimension of revelation that the other aspects of teaching do not flow in. Teachers, I cannot stress to you enough that worship must be a part of your Christian lifestyle.

Next, we see that they were given to **fasting**. One of the facets of fasting is that it draws us closer to God so that we can hear God clearly as he speaks to us. Also, as **Teachers**, we need to be able to speak the Word of God clearly to others. **Many start off being doctrinally correct but often get side tracked with erroneous teachings, and we wonder how they got way over into the left field.** Probably, because **they did not have a lifestyle that was committed to ministering to the Lord through fasting and praying** in order to seek the face of God and His strategy. So, the **Teacher** must not only minister to the Lord but must also have a prayer and fasting lifestyle.

Lastly, as part of the Church leadership, we see the Teacher was one of the team that laid hands. There are several instances in the New Testament where we see the laying on of hands. One instance is to convey the gifts of the spirit and another is to endorse a person who has been chosen by God to do a work. In this text we see the Prophets and Teachers gifts working together.

Here we have two unique combinations of "anointings" collaborating to give birth to a ministry. They laid hands on Paul and Barnabas to convey the "giftings" they had to these two and to induct them in their Apostleship. This is both Apostolic and Prophetic in nature and I have devoted an entire chapter to talk about the Apostolic and **Prophetic Teacher**. Keep in mind this is not where you may necessarily start off, but if you are a part of modern-day Church of Antioch, this is what you will ultimately develop into.

I am not sure what your picture of the **Teacher** was before, but if it was just a person that teaches children's school in church on a Sunday or even a Bible Study, as you can see the New Testament Modern-day **Antioch gift of Teacher** is much more! God has more! Do you want it? Keep reading!

Ceretta Smith

Lesson 2 Notes

33

Lesson 2 Notes

Lesson 3

Lesson from Apollos the Teacher

One example of a New Testament Teacher from the Bible that I want us to look at is Apollos. He had the gift of the Teacher so, let us see what scripture has to say about him and his ministry — **Act 18:24-28:**

"And a certain Jew named Apollos, born at Alexandria, an eloquent man, and mighty in the scriptures, came to Ephesus.

25This man was instructed in the way of the Lord; and being fervent in the spirit, he spake and taught diligently the things of the Lord, knowing only the baptism of John.

26And he began to speak boldly in the synagogue: whom when Aquila and Priscilla had heard, they took him unto them, and expounded unto him the way of God more perfectly.

27And when he was disposed to pass into Achaia, the brethren wrote, exhorting the disciples to receive him: who, when he was come, helped them much which had believed through grace:

28For he mightily convinced the Jews, and that publicly, shewing by the scriptures that Jesus was Christ."

Now, there are several things we can ascertain from this text above. In verse 24, we learn that Apollos was eloquent, meaning he was learned; he was a man of letters, skilled in literature and the arts. He was also specially versed in history and the antiquities and had the skill of good public speaking. As **Teachers**, we have to study and expand our vocabulary in order to be effective public speakers. For example, you may need to take some classes and learn about the history and culture of those whom you are teaching about. You may need to take a Greek or Hebrew class; however the Lord leads you, but as **Teachers**, we are held to a higher standard as was the case with Apollos.

Next in verse 25, we see that he had been instructed or taught himself in the things of God and that he taught (**Didasko**). **We that are Teachers always have to remain teachable.** We can never get too prideful and think that we know it all. In the case of Apollos, as a result of what he had been taught coupled with his zeal and passion, he went about teaching others and he did it effectively. As stated in

scriptures, Apollos refreshed and revived believers with his teaching gift. We should also refresh and revive the body of Christ with our teaching gift. Our gifts should always point people back to God concerning their lifestyle and service to God.

In verse 26, we find Apollos in the synagogue boldly expounding the Gospel. But what he was teaching was that the Messiah was coming, but as we keep reading we find that there was one problem with what he was teaching. He and his teachings were behind the times; meaning that his teaching was not sound. As **Teachers**, our teaching is built upon the foundation of Christ and the foundation of truths that are laid by the Apostles and Prophets as stated in Ephesians 2:20.

Teachers, we have to stay on the cutting edge! And staying on the cutting edge will cost you; yes, it is going to cost you your time, your energy and yes, your money! We have to position ourselves and make sure we are upgrading ourselves as God is upgrading and shifting His church; God is shifting. This means that we will have to take continuing biblical education classes via a campus, seminars, or in a conference type setting.

More importantly we need to be under that Apostolic and Prophetic covering and a part of that team we saw earlier in the Antioch Church. Do not fret, we have all missed the mark at one time or another and had to go back or revisit some areas where we taught something that was not correct. Be encouraged because, there was help for Apollos and there is help for you and me today. Aquila and Priscilla (a husband and wife team in ministry) were present during one of Apollos' teaching sessions and noticed his errors. They took Apollos aside and they properly informed him that the Messiah had come, that the prophecies had been fulfilled, and that Jesus had died and rose from the dead and they shared with him the gift of the Holy Spirit. Once Apollos learned a more excellent way, he went forth with even more zeal and vigor to help others to believe.

Teachers should always be open and submitted to someone in authority over you. If your heart is pure and your motives are for the advancement of God's Kingdom, God will not allow you to walk around in error. He will send someone to teach you a more excellent way. It may be your leaders, another **Teacher** or better yet; the Holy Spirit! As **Teachers**, we have to stay plugged into the Holy Spirit so that we can always walk in the more excellent way. There are many Apollos' out there and I hope that this book will do for them what Aquilla and Priscilla did for Apollos. It is not enough to have zeal and vigor; with it must come truth!

I decree the gift of the **Teacher** be stirred up in you and that you go forth with the zeal and passion as Apollos and Paul and that you teach the Word of God with the power of the Holy Spirit. May the revealed truth of God's Word flow from the deep recesses of your spiritual being and bring light to darkness, clarity to cloudiness, freedom to bondage, and certainty to all the uncertain in Jesus' name! Amen, amen, amen!

Ceretta Smith

Lesson 3 Notes

Lesson 3 Notes

Lesson 4

Jesus the Master Teacher; Our Greatest Example

The Lord as the ultimate example of the teacher is evidenced in the following scriptures:

Matthew 5:22:

"But I say unto you, That whosoever is angry with his brother without a cause shall be in danger of the judgment: and whosoever shall say to his brother, Raca, shall be in danger of the council: but whosoever shall say, Thou fool, shall be in danger of hell fire."

Matthew 9:35:

"<u>And Jesus went about all the cities and villages, teaching in their synagogues</u>, and preaching the gospel of the kingdom, and healing every sickness and every disease among the people."

Luke 13:22:

"<u>And he went through the cities and villages, teaching</u>, and journeying toward Jerusalem."

Jesus walked in all of the five-fold ministry gifts and He is our greatest example of a Teacher and there are many lessons that we can learn from the Master Teacher. Now, I am going to hit on a few lessons that I think will jump-start you concerning your gift to teach but they are by no means the only lessons to be learned but I think that they will be an excellent Bible Study for you to do independently.

The Importance of Submission

The first lesson we can draw from in Jesus' teaching ministry was the source of His power. Jesus was totally and completely submitted to His Father God and God was the source of His power. Jesus did nothing outside of the will of the Father and His teachings lined up completely with the will of the Father. As we discussed in the previous chapter, the life of the teacher must be given to ministering to the Lord Jesus and he or she must always envelope what he or she does with prayer. That is how the Lord Jesus was able to stay on target. Any moment that the source of our gifting becomes someone or something other than the Holy Spirit, we need to repent quickly and get back in line with the will and voice of God. We have to make sure that we are completely submitted to the will God and not teach what we want to teach, but teach what God's Word says.

God will always place us under the authority of His divine leadership. Always remember that God's order is, firstly Apostles, secondarily Prophet and thirdly Teacher. We have to make sure that within the local churches we are submitted to the men and women of God who are the leaders. As the Apostles lay the foundations and give instructions on what we are to teach the people, these foundations become the platform on which we are to build upon in our teaching. As they give us the areas that we are to instruct or teach on, the Holy Spirit will give us the plans on how to deliver the Word so that the people will understand it, grab it and apply it to their everyday lives. Therefore, the first lesson we can learn from the **Master Teacher** is that of submission.

Methodology

The next lesson we can learn from the Master Teacher is methodology. Jesus used a variety of methods when He was teaching. He are a few of them:

1. The Question Method

One method that Jesus used was **"the question method"** of teaching. He asked His disciples in Matthew 16:16, "Whom do men say that I, the son of man am?" As you can see, He posed a question that allowed Him to make an assessment of where the people were concerning their understanding of Him. By doing this, He could then tailor His messages and teaching to best suit those He was trying to reach. Jesus often used the question method to answer a question in order to draw his student to a clearer understanding of the message He was trying to convey.

2. Lecture Method

Another method Jesus used was the **"lecture method"** of teaching and a good example of which is the *"Sermon on the Mount"* in Matthew chapters 5-7. This method of teaching allowed Jesus to have control over what He was teaching and it also gave Him room to tailor the materials to His listener. This method is more structured and is not a method I would suggest you use for teenagers.

3. Story Telling or Parables Method

A third method Jesus used to teach was story **"telling or parables."** A parable simply put is an earthly story that has a heavenly meaning. Jesus was able to keep the attention of His audience through these parables because they allowed the listeners to grab a hold to some deep truths. When I think of the 21st century teachers who employ this method, Joel Osteen comes to mind. He executes this method very well.

4. Spontaneous Method

The Lord Jesus was also a **spontaneous teacher**. An example of this would be when the adulterous woman was about to be stoned and they brought her to the Lord Jesus. During this event or encounter with those who sought to live by the LAW, He was able to teach a lesson with only one sentence; **"He without sin let him cast the first stone."** My God! The men went away with a clear understanding of God's GRACE. But even then His teaching was not done; He was able to teach the woman also of her self-worth and He commanded her to lay away the sin that was setting her back. **Teachers**, we have to be ready at all times because you never know when that door of opportunity will open for you to use one sentence to teach a lesson that will bring a lifetime of deliverance! Hallelujah!

5. The Example Method

The last method that Jesus used to teach was the **"example method"** of teaching. Jesus' whole life became an example for the whole human race. He made it a point to live the way that He wanted us to live. He was not only a hearer and teacher of the Word, but He was a doer also. **Teachers,** we have to be doers of the Word because people are watching and most importantly, God is watching!

Lesson 4 Notes

Lesson 4 Notes

Lesson 5

Characteristics of the Teacher

Have you ever asked yourself why you act a certain way or function a certain way? With certain "giftings," there are certain characteristics that are common regardless of race, gender or age. This is true of the Teaching gift as well.

The Teacher lives to learn and to teach. Not all will stand at a podium and teach but, there are some who will pen what they have learned into books, newspaper columns, magazine articles and even web sites. For these types of **Teachers,** writing will be the medium through which they teach. **Teachers love the Word of God and enjoy reading and are creative, imaginative and they enjoy teaching groups.** Overall, **Teachers** are confident, self-disciplined and can be sometimes technical. Most Teachers love to use graphs, lists and charts; research is your middle name. Teachers love to research and they enjoy studying. "Are you going… that's me, that's me!

A true Teacher's pet peeve is to see scriptures used out of context. Sometimes, our concern with accuracy can cause us to dwell on trivial things which in turn can cause us to be too detailed. There is a dimension of the perfectionist that we have to watch for and generally if we are yielded to the Holy Spirit, He will bring the balance that we need.

This ministry gift is not limited to teaching just the Bible; however the Bible is our yard stick for everything we teach. You may be one in a church, secular or workplace that God uses to teach on business, finance, leadership, and education to name a few, but the Bible still has to be your frame of reference. We had such a person in a ministry that I was a part of. She taught on finances and business but she always made sure that what she was teaching lined up with the Word of God. You many enjoy writing or being someone who develops various types of curriculums for teaching in a Bible Institute or a correspondence course instructor but you still have to make the Bible your foundation. As you are doing this, just know that with this gift, God will make room for you somewhere.

Ceretta Smith

Lesson 5 Notes

Lesson 5 Notes

Lesson 6

Practical Principles to Enhance Your Gift

Learning Styles

As God began to use my leaders to polish my gift, one of the things that I was introduced to was **Learning Styles**. Now, I had never heard about learning styles and I did not have a clue as to what this was, but, I can truly say that the understanding of this tool has helped me in the area of teaching.

I stated in a previous chapter that we need to know our audience. If you are a singer and you get hired to sing at a country western party and you show up and sing techno, your audience is not going to be engaged but disengaged. It is the same when we teach; we have to know how to reach each person that is in our audience. Understanding the learning styles will help you do just that. First, there is the Visual Learners.

1. **Visual Learner**

   These types of learners need to be able to see the teacher's body language and the teacher's facial expressions to be able to understand the lesson. These learners like to sit at the front of the class so that nothing is blocking their view. You would benefit this type of learner by incorporating pictures, visual displays, diagrams, handouts with illustrations and if you have the technology; power point or overhead transparencies. Next you have your Auditory Learners.

2. **Auditory Learners**

   This group learns from listening. They learn best through verbal lectures, having discussions, listening to what others have to say or by talking things through. The tone, pitch, and speed of your voice all influence this type of learner. These learner benefits from reading text aloud. Incorporating times to have someone read the text during a Bible Study would benefit these types of learners. And the last type of learner is the tactile/Kinesthetic Learners.

3. **Tactile/Kinesthetic Learner**

These learners learn through moving, touching and doing. These learners learn best through a hands-on approach. These learners find it hard sometimes to sit still for long periods and can become distracted by their need for activity. You would benefit these types of learners in your Bible Study by having skits where you ask for volunteers. They will jump at the chance to get out of their seat and explore the Word with you.

Have a Target

While knowing the learning styles can prove beneficial to adding flavor to your lessons, there are some other areas that I want to touch on as well. The first is **focusing your topic.** Make sure you are not all over the place concerning your topic but have a specific topic and you transition from point to point with a clear beginning and ending of your chosen topic. Preparing an outline is a good way to accomplish this.

Another thing that I like to do is, at the end of each block of instruction, I have the people repeat back to me each point and define what that point means. The art of learning is repetition and this also helps you to see if there is a point you need to reiterate.

Your Enthusiasm or Entheos

Next, be enthusiastic about what you are teaching. We are not entertainers and that is not what we are in ministry for, but if you are not excited about your lesson, the people will not be either. Think back to a class or Bible Study that you were in and you felt that the class was very boring so every five minutes, you looked at your watch prayed that it will be over soon. At some point, I have been on both ends of that picture and that is okay because it is all about learning and growing but your passion for the Word and what you are teaching should be evident and demonstrative.

Use of Technology

If you have the technology available and you are a Power Point fan like I am, here are some useful pointers that will help you prepare those presentations. First, let us talk

about font size; for a large audience, use a font that is size 18 or greater. If you have a small audience, use a font that is size 14 or greater. You also want to use a **sans-serif font** like <u>Helvetica</u>. Now, you are probably saying, *"What in the world is a sans-serif font?"* It is okay, I said the same thing when I first heard it. **A sans-serif font is a font that does not have the small features called "serifs" at the end of strokes.** Note the difference in the letters of the first and second fonts below. The tips of the latter fonts are curved.

AaBbCc

AaBbCc

You may be saying what is the difference? Does it really matter? The difference is that for printed reports and so forth, the **serif fonts** like <u>Times Roman</u> look very nice but these fonts will cause blurring and eye strain when they are projected. So, to answer the question; yes, it does make a difference.

Okay, we have talked about font and font size; now let us look at colors. This one is a hard one for me to stick to because I love colors, but the rule is not to use colors to make your presentations pop unless you are trying to emphasize a point. By nature, the human eye is drawn to changes in colors so using colors can be good when you are trying to emphasize a point but if you use colors everywhere, it will cause your presentation to look cluttered and also disrupt your listener's concentration.

An example of this would be to color chronological bullets in different colors so that your presentation has variance. Without knowing, this would be very distracting to your audience. An example of an effective way to use colors would be to use one color for your header topic and then use a different color for your bullets. In which case the change of color will highlight your header topic and draw your listener's eye to the header which is the first thing you want them to read.

When preparing slides, you should know that you need to limit the number of bullets that you put on your slides. Keep them at five or fewer. The first reason for this is to reduce clutter and the second is that most people cannot hold more than five to seven

items in their short term memory. By limiting your bullets to five or less, this will ensure that the majority of the people in your audience will remember them. Also, make sure your bullets are short and snappy and avoid using complete sentences unless you are defining a word.

Another good fact to know is that most people read all the text on the slide before they give you their attention. So, the more text you have the longer it will take for the people to focus on you. Whenever it is possible, use pictures to emphasize your points rather than text. They say, "A picture is worth a thousand words" and it is true because it will allow you to use words to explain the picture. You can then target your intended audience such as your <u>visual</u> and <u>auditory</u> learners. Be sure that your pictures reinforce your point because the use of random pictures will only distract your listeners.

Length of Presentation

The last area that I want to cover is the length of your lesson. The average attention span of an adult and a teenager is 20 minutes long according to various studies that have been done. The next time you attend a class or some type of lecture at about the 25 minute mark, start to observe the people. You will see people doodling, reading papers, passing notes, sleeping, texting, and if you are in a college setting, you may even see them searching the web on their computers.

With this in mind the average time for a lesson should be around 50 minutes. Now, having said that; let me say this. We are not a programmed church because the Holy Spirit must always have the liberty to change the program. So, yes, if the Spirit of God is flowing or moving in your teaching session, that is a different scenario but this move will be evident to you and your leaders and they will give you the liberty to keep flowing when this is the case. But, for general purposes, 50 to 60 minutes should allow you to teach a good solid lesson.

The "Change-up" Tool

Research has also shown that after those first 20 minutes, people start to disengage, so we have to add what they call a "change-up" in our lesson at the 20 minute mark to restart the attention clock of our audience again. Variety is a powerful tool; use it to your advantage and for your students' benefit. The "change-up" can be you telling them a story, a skit, a praise break with a song, a demo that you have put together, or a break if you are in a setting where you can do that. The objective is to do something that will give

the brain a break. On that note, I think I'll give your brain a break on this topic. There is such a plethora of resources on this subject out there, so take what I've given you and look for resources to help you build a good solid teaching foundation.

Ceretta Smith
Lesson 6 Notes

Lesson 6 Notes

Lesson 7

The Apostolic and Prophetic Teacher

In an earlier chapter we talked about what this teacher does and I touched on it briefly but I did not really go into depth. I would like to devote this chapter to talking specifically about the **Apostolic and Prophetic Teacher. Apostles are Teachers and most Prophets are also Teachers, but not all Teachers are Apostles or Prophets.** However, if connected to these gifts, there is a dimension of these gifts the Teacher can flow in.

Ready set, jump of that diving board; here we go! One of the functions of the Apostle is to lay the foundation and that foundation is the revelation of Jesus Christ. Many times in laying the foundation, they have to deal with false belief systems and correct error. I stated previously that all Apostles are Teachers but not all Teachers are Apostles. However, if you are connected to an Apostle and if he or she sends you out as a Teacher to minister to the body of Christ in your local area or even to the nations; along with being sent, comes a measure of "apostolic grace" that you will flow in as you teach. This will also depend on the sphere of influence God has called you to.

The "apostolic grace" will allow you to administrate and execute your teaching with an anointing that can only come from an impartation that is birthed out of covenant relationship. Without this "apostolic grace," it can be difficult to go into places and build on foundations and instruct the truth. Priscilla and Aquilla are biblical examples of those who received the "apostolic grace." Paul lived with them for about eighteen months and they traveled with the Apostle Paul helping him in ministry and they helped to establish a church.

The Apostle Paul mentions that this couple even risked their lives to save his and this shows that they had to be in a covenant relationship. They were both "mentees" (students) of the Apostle Paul and both were teachers in their own right. As recorded in **1 Corinthians 16:19**, they had a church in their home. Through that covenant relationship, a dimension of the apostolic grace that was upon the Apostle Paul's life was imparted to them; they were able to teach and firmly establish the church in Ephesus.

If you endeavor to move to this next level, seek God in prayer for that apostolic dynamic and from who this type of covenant relationship is to come. There is power in covenant!

The Prophetic Teacher

Now, we have talked a about the Apostolic dimension, let us look at the **Prophetic Teacher** dimension. First, let us look at some of the functions of the **Prophet**. Prophets reveal the Rhema Word, inspire the spirit, move by revelation, and move as the Holy Spirit leads while communicating what God is saying. Now, these are not all the things they do, but for the point of the **Prophetic Teacher**, these are the things I want to accent. Most Prophets are Teachers, but not all Teachers are Prophets, again the dual gifting will be noted if this is the case. Therefore, we have to be balanced and know our spheres of authority.

As I said before, the **Teacher** can flow in a measure of the prophetic when teaching as prompted by the Holy Spirit. A **Prophetic Teacher** can and will move in the area of releasing a Rhema Word and that Word will inspire the spirits of the people. That does not mean you are a Prophet. This is especially prevalent in ministries that embrace the office of the Prophet and a company of Prophets or Prophetic Teams are being raised up. Teachers can and should move by revelation and move as the Holy Spirit leads.

The **Prophetic Teacher** should have times in their ministry when the Spirit of God just downloads a revelation to them on the spot or times that a Rhema Word comes forth. It is usually in the form of a Word of wisdom or a Word of knowledge. It is not anything in your notes, not anything you studied or rehearsed, not information given to you by another person, but suddenly a Word just bubbles up; I call it a "I don't how I got on this, it wasn't in my notes, but here we Go moment!" I usually just let the Holy Spirit have at it. Now, we do know how we get into those flows; it is the Holy Spirit, but the point is that it is not something that you had knowledge of prior to your ministering the Word.

A simple example of this would be something that happened to me recently. I was teaching a Bible Study on prayer and one of the points that I was making was, being specific in what you want from God. I then began to use the example of a single woman who wanted a husband and the Holy Spirit just really began to flow and it seemed to open up something for me to address in detail so I stayed there until I felt the Holy Spirit release me from the Word.

After service, I had several single women come up to me and they said that God had been dealing with them on the very things that the Holy Spirit had ministered through me. Again, a Word of Knowledge was released to the single women while I was teaching. We do not *know* what *ledge* some people are on but God does and if we will speak what we hear; even when we are teaching, lives will be touched and people will get the answers they have been seeking. We have to be sensitive and shift when God says to shift.

How many times have you been in an audience of a church service or conference and the minister started to speak directly to an issue you were dealing with at that time; if you did not know better, you would think that the minister had been at your house or in your car listening to your conversations. Well, they were not but God was and what happened was the prophetic dimension was flowing and operating.

In closing, I will say that if you are not flowing in these dimensions as a Teacher in the body of Christ, then you need to seek God in prayer and ask Him to point you in the direction of a true <u>School of the Prophets</u> or the <u>School of the Apostles</u>. These schools will educate you, activate you and impart to you the necessary anointing so that you can begin to walk in the fullness of your gift with demonstration. But, again, be prayerful because there are so many counterfeits out there but the good steps of a righteous man have been ordered and God by His Spirit will lead you.

Lesson 7 Notes

Ceretta Smith

Lesson 7 Notes

Lesson 8

Warning to Teachers

The Bible gives a clear warning to the Teacher and I think it is important to include the warning in this book. **Teachers,** we have an awesome responsibility and it should not be taken lightly.

James 3:1:

"Not many of you should become teachers (*Didaskalos*), my fellow believers, because you know that <u>we who teach will be judged more strictly</u>."

The Powerful Influence of the Teacher

This text lets us know that the Teacher will be judged more strictly. Why is this you may be asking? **The answer is because Teachers influence the lives of their hearers.** We teach with the purpose of trying to transform a mind by renewing it, or introduce a new way of thinking to the mind. Either way, what we teach will influence our listeners because people usually act on what they hear; that is why teaching cannot be taken lightly.

Pitfalls of the Teacher

There are two areas I want to stress in this final chapter that we as five-fold ministry gift — **Teachers**, need to be aware of for therein lays the potential for pitfalls for us.

1. **Acceptance and Rejection**

   The first area is in the **acceptance and rejection of the materials** that we use to teach. I have seen and heard of many that have fallen into deception in this area. As we are studying and preparing lesson to teach, our foundation and measuring stick must always be the Bible. Listen, there is so much out there on the web and in our Christian bookstores; you have to be able to discern what is not of God. It

is our responsibility to filter out the bad and walk in and teach the truth. It can happen to the best of us because none of us is exempted from it, but if we will guard this gate of our ministry, we will be successful.

2. **Pride**

Another area is **pride**. **Teachers**, this is real and I say again that none of us is exempt. A major vulnerability of being a **Teacher** is that we can swell up with pride. **Teachers** can sometimes feel that they have an advantage over their brothers and sisters in the Church. This is so far from the truth because the truth is that the ability to teach is a gift and the Holy Spirit is the one who opens our spiritual eyes and ears to hear and see those things in the Word of God. The anointing is not for us but for God's people and we are to share what we learn with the Church. Always remember that God resist the proud, but gives grace to the humble. Therefore, we must check ourselves to make sure we are walking in humility and not pride.

Ceretta Smith

Lesson 8 Notes

Ceretta Smith

Lesson 8 Notes

Ceretta Smith

Lesson 8 Notes

Conclusion

It is my prayer that this teaching guide has been a blessing to you and that as a result of reading it, you have a greater understanding of the five-fold ministry gift of **Teacher**. I pray the words on these pages will enhance your ministry and that you reach your full potential as a **Teacher**. I want to close by decreeing some things over your life and ministry.

In the name of Jesus, I decree that no weapon formed against your **Teachers** will prosper. I decree that truth will flow from their loins and that spiritual discernment will be your guard. I decree that in all your getting, that you get an understanding of the Word and teach it with clarity and simplicity to your people. I decree the anointing that makes teaching easy is your portion.

God, I decree that even from these pages, a divine impartation and activation is taking place in the lives and ministries of the readers and that the Apostolic and Prophetic dimensions of their gift to **Teach** is stirred up right now in the name of Jesus. I call it forth and decree that gestation has begun and that it will be birthed at the appointed time. I decree increase in revelation as they give themselves to study Your Word and show themselves approved to You Lord; workmen that are not ashamed, but rightly divide Your Word.

I decree that their gift will make room for them and doors are opening now in Jesus' name. I decree that their foundation is built upon the Word of God and that the Word is their spiritual measuring stick and that every false doctrine of the enemy will be exposed. I decree a new level of boldness and confidence upon them in Jesus' name. I decree that the weapons of their warfare are not carnal but mighty through You God to the pulling down of strongholds. I decree that they will go into fortified places and tear down walls of religion and false doctrines with the truth of Your Word and that sons and daughters will be birthed into the Kingdom of God. I decree that it is so and that it is established this day in Jesus' name; Amen.

Bibliography

Barnes Notes on the Bible Definition on page 14, Studylight.org Greek and Hebrew Lexicons at www.studylight.org.

Dictionary.com page 15, www.ntlf.com/html/pi/9601/article1.htm.

TO HIS GLORY PUBLISHING COMPANY, INC.

463 Dogwood Dr. Lilburn, GA. 30047, U.S.A (770)458-7947

Order Form for Bookstores in the USA

Order Date: _____

Order Placed By: _____   By Fax: _____

Address: _____

_____

City _____ ST/ZIP _____

Phone #: _____

Email: _____

Purchase Order#: _____

Return Policy: Within 1 year but not before 90 Days.

Price	**Quantity**	**List Price**
Shipping Method:		
Media:		
UPS:		
FedEx:		
Other (Please Secify):		
Total Price:	**Total Quantity:**	**List Price**

Ship To Address: **Bill to Address:**